Thinking Critically: Fake News

Kathryn Hulick

San Diego, CA

© 2020 ReferencePoint Press, Inc.
Printed in the United States

For more information, contact:
ReferencePoint Press, Inc.
PO Box 27779
San Diego, CA 92198
www.ReferencePointPress.com

Picture Credits:
cover: bluecinema/iStockphoto.com
8: PeopleImages/iStock.com
Charts and graphs by Maury Aaseng

LIBRARY OF CONGRESS CATALOGING-IN-PUBLICATION DATA

Name: Hulick, Kathryn., author.
Title: Thinking Critically: Fake News/by Kathryn Hulick.
Description: San Diego, CA: ReferencePoint Press, Inc., 2019. | Series: Thinking Critically |
    Includes bibliographical references and index.
Identifiers: LCCN 2019007516 (print) | LCCN 2019007998 (ebook) | ISBN 9781682826607 (eBook)
    | ISBN 9781682826591 (hardback)
Subjects: LCSH: Fake news—Juvenile literature.
Classification: LCC PN4784.F27 (ebook) | LCC PN4784.F27 H85 2019 (print) | DDC 070.4/3—dc23
LC record available at https://lccn.loc.gov/2019007516

Contents

Foreword

"Literacy is the most basic currency of the knowledge economy we're living in today." Barack Obama (at the time a senator from Illinois) spoke these words during a 2005 speech before the American Library Association. One question raised by this statement is: What does it mean to be a literate person in the twenty-first century?

E.D. Hirsch Jr., author of *Cultural Literacy: What Every American Needs to Know*, answers the question this way: "To be culturally literate is to possess the basic information needed to thrive in the modern world. The breadth of the information is great, extending over the major domains of human activity from sports to science."

But literacy in the twenty-first century goes beyond the accumulation of knowledge gained through study and experience and expanded over time. Now more than ever literacy requires the ability to sift through and evaluate vast amounts of information and, as the authors of the Common Core State Standards state, to "demonstrate the cogent reasoning and use of evidence that is essential to both private deliberation and responsible citizenship in a democratic republic."

The *Thinking Critically* series challenges students to become discerning readers, to think independently, and to engage and develop their skills as critical thinkers. Through a narrative-driven, pro/con format, the series introduces students to the complex issues that dominate public discourse—topics such as gun control and violence, social networking, and medical marijuana. Each chapter revolves around a single, pointed question such as Can Stronger Gun Control Measures Prevent Mass Shootings?, or Does Social Networking Benefit Society?, or Should Medical Marijuana Be Legalized? This inquiry-based approach introduces student researchers to core issues and concerns on a given topic. Each chapter includes one part that argues the affirmative and one part that argues the negative—all written by a single author. With the single-author format the predominant arguments for and against an issue can be synthesized into clear, accessible discussions supported by details and evidence including relevant facts, direct quotes, current examples, and statistical illustrations. All volumes include focus questions to guide students as they read each pro/con discussion, a list of key facts, and an annotated list of related organizations and websites for conducting further research.

The authors of the Common Core State Standards have set out the particular qualities that a literate person in the twenty-first century must have. These include the ability to think independently, establish a base of knowledge across a wide range of subjects, engage in open-minded but discerning reading and listening, know how to use and evaluate evidence, and appreciate and understand diverse perspectives. The new *Thinking Critically* series supports these goals by providing a solid introduction to the study of pro/con issues.

Fake News

In a video, two men on a motorbike ride up to a group of children playing in the street. They grab a boy and ride off. In 2018 this alarming video and warnings to watch out for gangs of kidnappers spread through India on the social media messaging service WhatsApp. Fearful for their own children, a group of people from the village of Dhule attacked and killed five men they suspected of being kidnappers. In a separate incident in a different village, two men who stopped to ask for directions were killed for the same reason.

As it turned out, none of the men who died were kidnappers. Nobody was. The video was clipped from a longer video created to help prevent child abduction and trafficking in Pakistan. The original video was staged with actors. In the end, the child returned and one of the men held up a sign warning parents to be vigilant. The posts on WhatsApp about bands of kidnappers prowling the streets of India were fake news.

A Bounty of Bad Information

Fake news is a story that seems like real news but involves misleading, deceptive, or false information. Some experts define fake news narrowly as information that is entirely invented and spread with the intention to misinform people. The motive behind this type of fake news may be to make money or to advance a political agenda. The term *fake news* can also be defined more broadly to include any type of bad information that some people wrongly accept as true.

For example, propaganda is information created to appeal to people's emotions and influence their opinions. It often involves misleading information, opinions, information taken out of context, or lies. Politicians

6

and advertisers both regularly use propaganda to try to build a base of supporters. Pseudoscience provides information that rejects or misrepresents science and scientific research. Misinformation includes myths and rumors. People who create and spread misinformation may not realize that the information is false or misleading. Clickbait is false or misleading information created to make money. And satires or hoaxes are fake information created to entertain. The creators usually do not intend to fool anyone, but some people may not get the joke. Fake news does not include opinions or critical reporting, unless those reports make an attempt to deceive. It does not include honest mistakes or errors that get corrected.

A Flurry of Fake News

Twisting the truth is not a modern invention. People have been spreading lies and propaganda through various media for thousands of years. In the past, false and misleading information could only spread through books, magazines, newspapers, radio, and television. Today, thanks to the Internet and social media, fake news can instantly reach a worldwide audience at almost no cost. And fake news often gets mixed together with real news in social media feeds and Internet search results. "Truth is no longer dictated by authorities, but is networked by peers," says Kevin Kelly, cofounder of *Wired* magazine. "For every fact there is a counterfact and all these counterfacts and facts look identical online, which is confusing to most people."[1]

The term *fake news* is relatively new. Craig Silverman, a reporter at BuzzFeed, began using the term as early as 2014 to describe stories circulating on the Internet that were completely false yet presented as true in a clear attempt to deceive. For example, one of the stories Silverman found in 2014 claimed that an entire town in Texas had been quarantined after

> "Truth is no longer dictated by authorities, but is networked by peers. For every fact there is a counterfact and all these counterfacts and facts look identical online, which is confusing to most people."[1]
>
> —Kevin Kelly, cofounder of *Wired* magazine

an Ebola outbreak there. This never actually happened. "It used a fake quote attributed to someone at a Texas hospital to pass itself off as a real news story,"[2] Silverman says. He tweeted out a warning, calling the story "fake news."

Silverman began to hunt down these types of stories. Whenever possible, he debunked the lies and exposed the people telling them. By November 2016, shortly before the US presidential election between Donald Trump and Hillary Clinton, Silverman's sleuthing led him to the town of Veles in Macedonia. There teenagers and young adults had created around 140 websites supporting then-candidate Trump. These young people would find a sensational story, which was often completely false, copy it to one of their websites, then post links on Facebook. Some of these posts received hundreds of thousands of shares, reactions, and comments. Every time someone clicked through to one of their web- sites, the young Macedonians made money from ads. "The Americans loved our stories and we make money from them. Who cares if they are true or false?"[3] says an anonymous nineteen-year-old Macedonian. Meanwhile, Russian operatives were also spreading fake news on social media. Except these agents had a political agenda. They wanted Trump to win the election.

Trump did win the election, and some wondered whether made-up news stories and other forms of bad information might have swayed the vote in his favor. Others thought fake news had very little impact, if any at all, on the outcome. A similar drama played out again in 2017 in Britain, when the country voted to leave the European Union, a decision known as Brexit. Once again, a slew of fake news and misinformation spread in advance of the vote. It is impossible to know for sure whether fake news about key issues in either of these two votes changed the outcome. But it is definitely true that these incidents and others like them have made people all over the world, regardless of their politics, sit up and notice fake news.

A Twist on the Term

Trump himself seized onto the idea of fake news. One reporter estimates that Trump tweeted about fake news over two hundred times in 2018. However, the president has twisted the meaning of the term. When Trump calls something or someone "fake news," it means that he does not like what that story or person is saying. In a tweet on May 9, 2018, he made this meaning very clear. He said, "The Fake News is working overtime . . . 91% of the Network News about me is negative (Fake)."[4] Most of the time, the reports he calls "fake" come from news outlets that

> "The Fake News is working overtime . . . 91% of the Network News about me is negative (Fake)."[4]
>
> —Donald Trump, president of the United States

strive to present real, reliable, well-sourced stories. For example, on November 30, 2017, the *New York Times* reported that Rex Tillerson, who was secretary of state at the time, would likely be forced out of office. The next day, Trump tweeted, "The media has been speculating that I fired

Rex Tillerson or that he would be leaving soon—FAKE NEWS!"[5] In March 2018, though, Trump fired Tillerson. So the original news report had been based on reliable sources. The fake news problem today therefore involves fake or misleading stories presented as truth as well as true stories unfairly labeled as fake.

What to Believe?

Fake news only causes a problem if people believe it. It may seem like people should be able to sniff out fake stories, like a rumor about salt curing Ebola that spread on social media during an outbreak in Nigeria in 2014. According to reports, two people died and around twenty others had to go to the hospital after consuming dangerously high amounts of salt. But even people who pride themselves on being aware fall for fake news. Strong emotions are one factor. Outrage, fear, disgust, surprise, or other strong emotions can cloud judgment and affect decision-making. This is likely what happened in the kidnapping tragedy in India as well as in the Ebola outbreak.

Existing personal or political beliefs also affect whether a person falls for fake news. People tend to believe information that supports what they already believe and ignore or mistrust information that goes against their beliefs. This is called confirmation bias. People are also more likely to go along with fake news when they are part of a larger group or crowd that is confirming the news. This is called groupthink. The effect takes place in the real world as well as in virtual groups on Facebook or Twitter.

Facing the Facts

All of this means that two people may interpret the exact same facts in very different ways. For example, after a controversial goal in a sports game, fans of one team will argue heatedly that the goal was fair, while fans of the other team will argue just as passionately that the goal should not count. All of the fans have access to the exact same factual information about the game. But that does not matter. The fans feel strong emotion about their team winning or losing. They have existing beliefs that their team is better. And they are part of a larger group that confirms their beliefs. So it is next to impossible for the fans to objectively and rationally analyze the goal.

Even when none of these factors come into play, it takes time and effort for a person to verify whether news is factual. People today are bombarded with news all the time. It is difficult to quickly tell the difference between well-researched stories, unsupported opinions, and outright lies. So fake news spreads alongside real news, confusing plenty of people into making decisions based on bad information.

Clearly, fake news is a problem. But the public disagrees on the scope of the problem and how it should be addressed.

Chapter One

Does Fake News Pose a Serious Threat?

Fake News Poses a Serious Threat

- Fake news has led to violent acts, hate crimes, and other harmful outcomes.
- Powerful leaders wield fake news to control public opinion.
- Fake news undermines democracy by making it more difficult for people to think independently.

The Debate at a Glance

Concerns About Fake News Are Exaggerated

- Fake news is nothing new. Civil society has survived similar problems in the past.
- Fake news does not reach a large enough audience to matter.
- Fake news has no real power to influence political outcomes.

Fake News Poses a Serious Threat

"We are all targets of disinformation, meant to erode our trust in democracy and divide us."

—Kate Starbird, professor, University of Washington

Quoted in University of Washington, "Understanding Fake News and Misinformation," May 29, 2018. www.washington.edu.

Consider these questions as you read:

1. Why might someone create fake news that incites hate and violence?
2. Why is controlling the news so important to authoritarian or totalitarian governments?
3. How does casting doubt on real news undermine democracy?

Editor's note: The discussion that follows presents common arguments made in support of this perspective, reinforced by facts, quotes, and examples taken from various sources.

Fake news is everywhere online, and people often have trouble telling it from factual reporting. Many fear what this might mean for the future of human society. People can only make well-informed, independent decisions if they have an accurate understanding of current events. Fake news clouds this understanding. When the powerful wield fake news in the form of propaganda or label real news as fake, they can manipulate public opinion. This may influence people to make a decision favorable to those in power—a decision people may not make if they have access to accurate information. In a democracy, this is not supposed to happen. All citizens, not a few powerful people, are supposed to determine policies. Fake news undermines democracy and threatens to destabilize society.

Inciting Violence and Hate Crimes

When fake news preys on strong emotions, it sometimes leads to very real and terrible consequences, such as the killings in India that resulted from false stories about child kidnappers. This horrible tragedy was not the first violent incident connected to fake news. In 2016, in response to a fake news story, Edgar Maddison Welch of North Carolina entered a pizza parlor in Washington, DC, armed with a semiautomatic rifle, shotgun, and knife. He fired several shots and searched the building, expecting to free enslaved children held in the basement. Supposedly, the children were part of a conspiracy masterminded by Hillary Clinton. But the conspiracy was a lie. The pizza parlor did not even have a basement. Thankfully, no one was hurt in this incident, which became known as "pizzagate." Soon afterward, Clinton said, "It's now clear that so-called fake news can have real-world consequences."[6]

> "It's now clear that so-called fake news can have real-world consequences."[6]
>
> —Hillary Clinton, former US secretary of state and 2016 US presidential candidate

Fake news or propaganda can also endanger entire groups of people or even fuel genocide. Propaganda targeting Jews and other minority groups helped make possible the horrors of the Holocaust during World War II. As another example, the number of Muslims who commit terrorist acts is a tiny percentage of the total population, and in the United States, non-Muslims are much more likely to commit terrorist acts. Yet anti-Muslim propaganda including false or misleading information is used to incite fear and hatred of all Muslims. In 2017 Donald Trump retweeted a series of anti-Muslim videos created by a political group in the United Kingdom. These types of messages may inspire real-life hate crimes, according to researchers at the University of Warwick. They found that when Trump sent a higher number of tweets related to Islam, a higher number of hate crimes targeting Muslims would occur in the days and weeks afterward, especially in places where many people use Twitter. The research does not prove that Trump's tweets cause people to commit hate crimes, but the correlation is disturbing.

Fake News Keeps Growing

Fake news continues to be a serious problem. In a 2018 study, researchers at the Massachusetts Institute of Technology looked at over 4.5 million tweets from 2006 through 2017. Of these, eighty thousand contained false claims, as identified by independent fact-checking organizations. Mapping those false tweets over time reveals that fake news is a growing problem, particularly on Twitter.

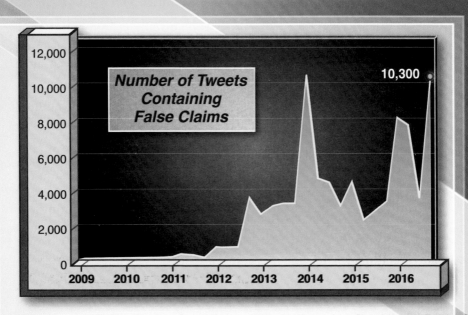

Number of Tweets Containing False Claims

10,300

Source: Steve Lohr, "It's True: False News Spreads Faster and Wider. And Humans Are to Blame," *New York Times*, March 8, 2018. www.nytimes.com.

This same drama is playing out all around the world. Campaigns of disinformation and fake news, mostly spread on social media, are contributing to unsafe conditions for marginalized or minority groups. In Myanmar today, genocide against the Rohingya is ongoing. To justify the violence, security forces distribute propaganda and fake news. In fact, the United Nations Independent International Fact-Finding Mission on Myanmar found that misinformation on Facebook helped cause the conflict.

Harmful Decisions

Most fake news stories do not have such concrete and dire real-world consequences. But fake news, propaganda, and pseudoscience often incite general feelings of anger or fear that may lead to harmful decisions. For example, fake news and pseudoscience have led some people to decide not to vaccinate themselves or their children. Vaccines are shots that protect a population from deadly diseases. Scientists and medical experts all agree that vaccination is safe and benefits society. However, in recent years groups of people who call themselves anti-vaxxers have spread fake news, propaganda, and misinformation trying to convince people that vaccination is harmful. To help combat this, YouTube has blocked anti-vaccination documentaries and Amazon has removed books on the subject from its online store.

Claire McCarthy, a pediatrician and American Academy of Pediatrics spokesperson, regularly has to try to persuade parents that vaccination is the right choice for their children. "When parents get scared, it's hard to un-scare them,"[7] she says. When enough parents decide not to vaccinate, a population suffers. In 2019 dozens of unvaccinated children in the state of Washington got the measles, a disease that can be deadly for very young kids. In this case and in other similar outbreaks, fear fueled by fake news led to kids coming down with a terrible disease.

A Weapon of Authoritarian Regimes

In totalitarian or authoritarian regimes, dictators manufacture the version of reality they want the people to believe. North Korea, for instance, uses propaganda and censorship to make it extremely difficult for its people to experience anything other than the government's version of truth. Russia regularly uses fake news campaigns to manipulate public opinion at home and abroad. For example, leading up to the 2016 US presidential election, Russian operatives spread fake news stories intended to make Clinton seem unfit to govern. She wound up losing the election, and fake news could be partially to blame.

A 2018 study by researchers at Ohio State University asked people who voted for Barack Obama in 2012 whether they believed several pro-Trump fake news stories that spread widely in 2016. Eighty-nine percent of the people who believed none of the stories voted for Clinton, but only 17 percent of those who believed two or three of the stories did. This correlation does not prove that fake news caused anyone to vote a certain way. But the study authors conclude, "It is highly likely that this pernicious pollution of our political discourse was sufficient to influence the outcome of what was a very close election."[8] Russia has attempted to influence public opinion in other countries as well. In 2017 British prime minister Theresa May spoke out against Russia's actions, saying that the country is "deploying its state-run media organizations to plant fake stories and photoshopped images in an attempt to sow discord in the West and undermine our institutions."[9]

> "It is highly likely that this pernicious pollution of our political discourse was sufficient to influence the outcome of what was a very close election."[8]
>
> —Richard Gunther, Paul A. Beck, and Erik C. Nisbet, researchers at Ohio State University

Undermining Democracy

Even in countries with more democratic ideals, powerful people regularly wield fake news as a weapon to distort the public's perceptions of reality. For example, tobacco companies used propaganda and misleading advertising for years to try to hide the fact that cigarette smoking leads to cancer and other serious health issues. Politicians routinely lie or make misleading statements in order to generate support for themselves and take support away from their opponents. Research has shown that repeating a lie again and again implants it in people's memories. Even if they disbelieve it the first time they hear it, they may later recall it as true.

To get people to believe the lies, it is not enough for a powerful person to spread falsehoods. It is also important to suppress or discredit the truth. Trump uses the term *fake news* to cast doubt on news media reporting that he does not like. Peter Wehner of the Ethics and Public Policy Center in Washington, DC, says, "The media has always been

> "A self-governing nation can't run if you can't have a common set of facts, if you can't agree on common realities."[11]
>
> —Peter Wehner of the Ethics and Public Policy Center

the institution in American life that has kept presidents accountable when it comes to what's true and what's not."[10] By attacking the media and spreading fear of fake news, Trump seems to be trying to set himself up as the only source of reliable information. He is telling people how to think rather than allowing them to think for themselves.

Yet his supporters trust him and believe what he says. Meanwhile, many of his opponents do not trust anything he says. Wehner says, "This has tremendous damaging effects on the political and civic culture of the country. A self-governing nation can't run if you can't have a common set of facts, if you can't agree on common realities."[11] In any country with democratic ideals, fake news and its close cousin, the manipulation of real news, each pose a serious threat.

Concerns About Fake News Are Exaggerated

"Personally I think the idea that fake news on Facebook, which is a very small amount of the content, influenced the election in any way—I think is a pretty crazy idea. Voters make decisions based on their lived experience."

—Mark Zuckerberg, chief executive officer of Facebook

Quoted in Casey Newton, "Zuckerberg: The Idea That Fake News on Facebook Influenced the Election Is 'Crazy.'" Verge, November 10, 2016. www.theverge.com.

Consider these questions as you read:

1. How do you think the impact of fake news in the past compares to its impact today?
2. Does it seem surprising that so many more people visit real news sites than fake news sites? Why do you think this is the case?
3. How persuasive is the argument that fake news has no real power to influence people's decisions?

Editor's note: The discussion that follows presents common arguments made in support of this perspective, reinforced by facts, quotes, and examples taken from various sources.

Fake news certainly seems alarming. And in rare cases, fake stories have directly led to violent acts. But true stories and facts can incite unnecessary violence and hatred as well. For example, it is a fact that many family planning clinics in the United States offer abortions. This fact has led some people who strongly oppose abortion to attack these clinics and the people who work there. Differences of opinion strong enough to inspire hatred will always exist and will make some people angry enough to act violently. Tragedies will happen with or without fake news.

Fake news is a normal part of free and open discourse and has been for centuries. It exists on the fringe of real news, with much less reach or power. Because of this, fake news is not a serious threat to democracy or civil society.

A Long History of Bad Information

Sensational headlines and invented stories have been helping sell media for centuries. Back in 1835 the *New York Sun* newspaper ran a hoax story about the discovery of life on the moon. The account included made-up quotes from one of the most well-respected astronomers of that time period. The creators of the story wanted to sell more papers, and the fake story did the trick. Satirical websites such as the *Onion* exist for this same reason. They churn out ridiculous stories because people love to read them—for entertainment, not factual information.

Fake news is much more concerning when the people behind it are trying to convince people to think a certain way. But it is important to understand that this type of fake news is also nothing new. In the late nineteenth century in America, the term *yellow journalism* referred to sensational reporting that skewed facts and promoted specific points of view. For example, when the ship the USS *Maine* sank in 1898, the *New York Journal* printed, without any evidence, that Spain had sunk the ship. Soon afterward, the Spanish-American War began. Investigators would later discover that the sinking was an accident. It may seem that this fake news started a war. But in fact, the two nations were already heading toward war. Yellow journalism did not and could not create conflict out of nothing. Rather, it responded to people's existing worries and fears.

This is exactly what happens today. When conflicts exist and emotions surrounding specific issues run high, some people, companies, or government officials will fabricate facts or exaggerate stories to support one side of the issue. Though fake news may worsen existing tensions, it is primarily a symptom of discord, not a cause. History shows that civil society can survive through an onslaught of misleading or entirely false news. The United States remained a democratic society despite the prominence of fake news in the nineteenth century. "Free and democratic societies generally right themselves before allowing propaganda to take them completely over the edge,"[12] writes Donald A. Barclay in his book *Fake News, Propaganda, and Plain Old Lies.*

Limited Reach

One very significant difference exists between past and current forms of fake news. Until recently, the Internet and social media did not exist. Some argue that these new media have created a fake news crisis.

However, fears of fake news on the Internet and social media have been overblown. Brand-new forms of media often inspire waves of moral panic. "The older generation warns against a new technology and bemoans that society is abandoning the 'wholesome' media it grew up with, seemingly unaware that this same technology was considered to be harmful when first introduced,"[13] writes Vaughan Bell, a psychologist at King's College in London. This pattern stretches back all the way to Socrates, who warned that writing would cause children to cease to use their memories and become forgetful. When radio was new, some adults feared that it would distract young people from reading. Television was initially feared to mark the end of radio, reading, and family conversation. And now social media, the newest communication technology, supposedly divides people, threatens society, and hides the truth. "Fake news became the new bogeyman in the era of social media and digital disruptions,"[14] says Matthew Fraser of the American University of Paris. As society adjusts to social media, the problems that seem so daunting now will not seem as terrible.

> "Free and democratic societies generally right themselves before allowing propaganda to take them completely over the edge."[12]
>
> —Donald A. Barclay, author of *Fake News, Propaganda, and Plain Old Lies*

Though it is true that fake news spreads more quickly and widely than real news on some social media platforms, real news remains far more prominent and popular. Several different groups of researchers have found that the audience for real news dwarfs the audience for fake news. A 2018 study in the journal *New Media & Society* looked at the reach of

The Audience for Real News Dwarfs the Audience for Fake News

Fake news stories, including one claiming that the Pope had endorsed Donald Trump for president (he had not), seemed rampant in the months leading up to the 2016 US presidential election. But even during this period, many more people were visiting real news websites and also spending more time looking at real news. This suggests that worries about the threat of fake news are overblown.

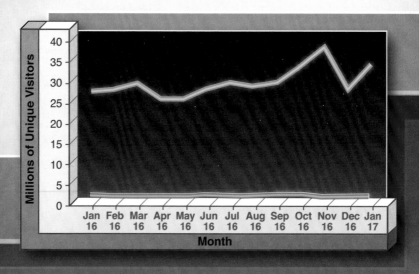

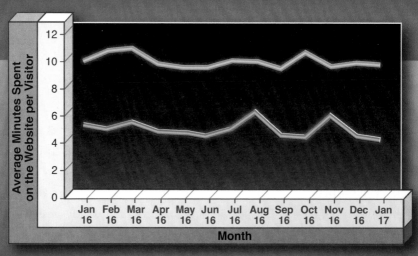

Fake News   Real News

Source: Hunt Alicott and Matthew Gentzkow. "Social Media and Fake News in the 2016 Election," *Journal of Economic Perspectives,* vol. 31, no. 2, Spring 2017. https://pubs.aeaweb.org.

fake news surrounding the 2016 US presidential election. The researchers found that from January 2016 through January 2017, the average real news website in the United States had 28 million unique visitors, while a fake news website had around 675,000 visitors. Most of the latter visitors arrived from links on Facebook. However, a 2019 study in the journal *Science* found that sharing links to fake news on Facebook is actually a rare activity. Just 8.5 percent of the people whose Facebook accounts the study looked at had shared at least one fake news article during 2016.

"For all the hype about fake news, it's important to recognize that it reached only a subset of Americans [during the 2016 election],"[15] says Brendan Nyhan of Dartmouth College, who led the *New Media & Society* study. Most of those Americans were already very loyal to a particular political party and also consumed a large amount of real news. This trend seems to hold true for other types of fake news in other countries. A 2018 study from the Reuters Institute for the Study of Journalism and the University of Oxford found that fake news in France and Italy reaches a very small segment of the population and that people also spend much less time looking at fake news than they do looking at real news.

> "For all the hype about fake news, it's important to recognize that it reached only a subset of Americans [during the 2016 election]."[15]
>
> —Brendan Nyhan of Dartmouth College

Limited Power

Research has also called into question whether fake news has any real power to sway people's opinions or affect decision-making. This is difficult to measure. But one research team compared the impact of fake news to the impact of television advertising on people's voting behavior. If exposure to one fake news item has the same effect as exposure to one television campaign ad, then the fake news leading up to the 2016 US presidential election would only have impacted votes by several hundredths of a single percentage point. That is not nearly enough to make a difference in the outcome.

It seems likely that the people who passed around fake news stories during the election had already made up their minds. Some may have shared these stories not because they believed them, but as a way to entertain their friends or demonstrate allegiance to their chosen candidate, suggest Duncan J. Watts and David M. Rothschild in a 2017 article for the *Columbia Journalism Review*. The authors conclude, "As troubling as the spread of fake news on social media may be, it was unlikely to have had much impact either on the election outcome or on the more general state of politics in 2016."[16] The same is likely to be true in connection with fake news campaigns intended to influence other populations around the world. The campaigns may rile people up but likely do not change very many people's minds.

> "As troubling as the spread of fake news on social media may be, it was unlikely to have had much impact either on the election outcome or on the more general state of politics in 2016."[16]
>
> —Duncan J. Watts and David M. Rothschild, *Columbia Journalism Review*

Fake news today seems like more of a symptom of a problem than a cause. The content exists to feed people's passion and outrage. These strong emotions would likely exist with or without the circulation of lies and misleading information. In fact, fake news can be viewed as a distraction that takes attention away from many more important divisive issues that face society.

Chapter Two

Does the News Media Tell the Truth?

The News Media Tries to Be Truthful

- Journalists are trained to act as objective observers and to convey facts.
- Mainstream media content is fact-checked and edited by others to ensure accuracy.
- Mainstream media are not infallible, but when they make errors they publicly correct them.
- Journalists serve the public by revealing truths that powerful people want to hide.

The Debate at a Glance

The News Media Has No Interest in Truth

- Subjective ideas and opinions lurk behind every news story.
- The news media skews facts to fit a specific point of view.
- Reaching the widest audience possible is more important to the media than truth.
- The news media helps powerful people cover up the truth.

The News Media Tries to Be Truthful

"I believe that clear thinking and clear statement, accuracy and fairness are fundamental to good journalism."

—Walter Williams, former dean of the Missouri School of Journalism

Walter Williams, "The Journalist's Creed," Missouri School of Journalism. https://journalism.missouri.edu.

Consider these questions as you read:

1. How can the media help ensure the freedom of opinion and information?
2. How persuasive is the argument that journalists go into the field to seek truth?
3. Which of the examples from the journalists' code of ethics seems most difficult to adhere to and why?

Editor's note: The discussion that follows presents common arguments made in support of this perspective, reinforced by facts, quotes, and examples taken from various sources.

In order for everyone in a society to have access to reliable, accurate information, someone needs to gather and distribute that information. Those responsible are the people who work for the news media: journalists, filmmakers, TV hosts, radio hosts, editors, publishers, and more. Reporting the news means telling the public the truth about what is going on in the world. Then the public is free to make well-informed decisions. The editorial board of Maine's *Portland Press Herald* puts it like this: "Our work is a search for the truth, and when we do it well, it's a crucial element of a system of government that makes an informed citizenry the ultimate authority."[17] A democracy can only work if people base their decisions on accurate, factual reporting.

Difficult and Dangerous Work

Journalists are the members of the news media on the front lines—often literally. They go to war zones, crime scenes, protests, and other places that may be dangerous. Some regularly put themselves in harm's way. In certain parts of the world, journalists are regularly attacked, jailed, or murdered for attempting to make the truth known. The Committee to Protect Journalists determined that in 2018, at least thirty-four journalists around the world were murdered, likely as retribution for their reporting. One of those killed was Jamal Khashoggi, a *Washington Post* columnist who criticized the royal family of Saudi Arabia.

Journalists often face tight deadlines or work nights and weekends to follow stories as they happen. And the profession is not highly paid. Despite the difficult and sometimes dangerous conditions of the job, people continue to work as reporters because they are committed to seeking true, meaningful stories.

> "Our work is a search for the truth, and when we do it well, it's a crucial element of a system of government that makes an informed citizenry the ultimate authority."[17]
>
> —*Portland (ME) Press Herald*

A Code of Ethics

Reporters usually go to school to study journalism. And once on the job, they often rely on organizations such as the Society of Professional Journalists (SPJ) or the American Press Institute for additional training and professional development. Educational programs in journalism teach students how to gather, assess, and present news fairly and accurately. For example, news is only as accurate as the sources it comes from. Primary sources—the people who lived the story or the experts behind a discovery or new idea—are essential. But a single primary source is not enough. Journalists are taught to independently seek other sources to confirm information.

Professional organizations require their members to uphold the ethics of the profession. The SPJ's code of ethics is a lengthy document with

Fact-Checking Is Growing Worldwide

The number of projects around the world that focus on fact-checking has more than tripled since 2014. In the United States, 87 percent of fact-checking projects are part of a larger news organization. Outside of the United States, independent entities often handle fact-checking. Either way, the numbers show that the media are devoted to truth and accuracy in their reporting.

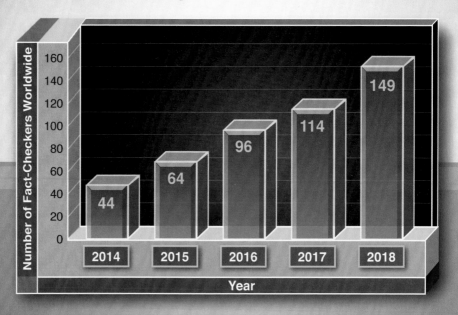

Source: Mark Stencel and Griffin Riley, "Fact-Checking Triples over Four Years," Duke Reporters' Lab, February 22, 2018. https://reporterslab.org.

four main sections. The first and longest section is titled "Seek the Truth and Report It." This section explains in great detail the many ways in which ethical journalists take care to provide accurate information. For example, the code says they should "use original sources whenever possible." They should also "support the open and civil exchange of views, even views they find repugnant." And they should "never deliberately distort facts or context, including visual information."[18]

Checking and Rechecking Facts

Of course, journalists are only human. They will not follow the highest ethical standards of the profession all of the time. They will slip up and make mistakes. But traditional news media has safeguards in place to try to catch errors. After a journalist submits a story, editors, fact-checkers, and copy editors get to work. These professionals are responsible for reviewing the story and making sure that the reporter not only got the facts right but presented them in a fair and objective manner. An editor may refuse to run a story if the sources of the information are not strong enough. The entire team must feel confident that the story is accurate and has merit.

Mistakes and errors do slip through, however, especially when an organization rushes to cover a breaking story. In an assessment of newspaper credibility, Scott R. Maier, a journalism professor at the University of Oregon, sent over four thousand articles to the sources quoted or mentioned in them to check for errors. The assessment found that 61 percent of the stories contained an error. Some of these errors were subjective; for example, overemphasizing part of a story. Objective errors such as mistaken dates or names were found in 48 percent of the stories.

Though these numbers seem high, most news organizations in the United States recognize that errors occur and have processes in place to correct mistakes. NBC News, ESPN, the *Washington Post*, the *New York Times*, and many other organizations have a page on their websites devoted to corrections. They also provide contact forms or email addresses that readers can use to point out errors. Media organizations take steps like this because they care about providing readers with fact-based, true stories.

Online publishing makes it possible to overwrite an error with a correction, but the industry standard is to always clearly explain the mistake that was made and corrected. At the *New York Times*, senior editor for standards Greg Brock and his team focus solely on corrections. "We never change a factual error online without telling readers that we've done it,"[19] says Brock. Craig Silverman, a journalist and author of the book *Regret the Error*, says that people do not lose confidence in a news organization when they see corrections noted. "It actually helps build confidence because people know we screw up so we'd better be acknowledging it,"[20] Silverman says. Public corrections make it clear that a news organization is not looking to hide or obscure anything, even its own mistakes.

Some news media organizations also seek to correct others' mistakes. Fact-checking projects may be affiliated with major news organizations or may be independent businesses or nonprofits. They look into statements by political figures, corporate executives, and others in power, and some also watch for rumors and misinformation on social media. The number of fact-checking projects has been steadily growing worldwide. These projects counteract fake news with facts.

An Enemy of the People?

Donald Trump has repeatedly lashed out at major media organizations in the United States, including CNN, the *New York Times*, and others. In July 2018 he tweeted, "The FAKE NEWS media (failing @nytimes, @CNN, @NBCNews and many more) is not my enemy, it is the enemy of the American people. SICK!"[21] Afterward, the *Boston Globe* organized a response from over four hundred news organizations around the United States. Each published its own editorial stating its commitment to accurate, true reporting and explaining the importance of a free press. The *Darien Times* of Connecticut stated, "Real news is our obligation. . . . This is not to say there aren't media outlets who are biased, and who attempt to distort and manipulate. But those are the few. We who believe are the many . . . we are the enemies of those who would seek to hide the truth from you."[22]

> "Real news is our obligation . . . We are the enemies of those who would seek to hide the truth from you."[22]
>
> —*Darien Times*

Yes, some people produce and distribute fake, misleading content.

But most news media organizations have very high standards and strong ethical foundations. The *Guardian*, a British newspaper, is clear about its mission: "We will give people the facts, because they want and need information they can trust, and we will stick to the facts. We will find things out, reveal new information and challenge the powerful."[23] When people make sure to go to this type of source for their news, they can trust that what they read or watch is true.

> "We will give people the facts, because they want and need information they can trust, and we will stick to the facts."[23]
>
> —Katharine Viner, editor in chief of the *Guardian*

The News Media Has No Interest in Truth

"Objective and unbiased journalism seems like the mythical unicorn—we've all heard of it but who has really ever seen it?"

—Najwa Shabir, editor, *Kashmir Observer*

Najwa Shabir, "Ideal Journalism—Does It Exist?," *Kashmir Observer* (Srinagar, India), April 28, 2016. https://kashmirobserver.net.

Consider these questions as you read:

1. Do you think it is possible to report the news without bias? Why or why not?
2. Do Americans have good reasons to mistrust the news media? Explain your answer.
3. How does competition for readers, viewers, and advertisers affect media efforts to be truthful and accurate?

Editor's note: The discussion that follows presents common arguments made in support of this perspective, reinforced by facts, quotes, and examples taken from various sources.

In an ideal world, the news media provides objective, unbiased, factual reporting. While many news organizations and journalists may strive to achieve this lofty goal, they rarely reach it. Too often, the truth takes a backseat to other, stronger incentives such as cooperating with private interests, avoiding unwanted backlash and criticism, or reaching a wide audience with an exciting story. Journalist Cynthia Crossen writes, "The media are willing victims of bad information, and increasingly they are producers of it. They take information from self-interested parties and add to it another layer of self-interest—the desire to sell information."[24]

Ulterior motives, subjective beliefs, biases, and opinions lurk behind almost every news story.

A Lack of Trust

The public is well aware of the media's ethical issues. Multiple studies assessing people's levels of trust in the media reveal a downward trend. For example, a 2016 Pew Research Center study found that only around 20 percent of Americans put a lot of trust in their local and national news organizations. A Gallup poll that same year recorded its lowest ever level of trust in the media's accuracy and fairness. In a 2018 survey conducted by the Knight Foundation and Gallup, 69 percent of American adults said their trust in the news media had decreased over the past decade. When asked why, respondents answered that the news media was biased and inaccurate. People were also less likely to trust news outlets that leaned toward political views that opposed their own beliefs.

Even back in 1995, long before the term *fake news* took off, experts were concerned about a lack of truth in the media. That year Peter Vanderwicken, a journalist and former head of corporate communication for a financial company, wrote an article for the *Harvard Business Review* titled "Why the News Is Not the Truth." He argued that the version of reality the press puts forward is manufactured by the government and powerful companies to sway public opinion. In other words, all media is propaganda, a form of fake news. "The news media and the government have created a charade that serves their own interests but misleads the public,"[25] he said, arguing that both the government and company officials promote the version of reality that they want the public to believe, and the news media goes along with it. In addition, private interests often manipulate

> "The media are willing victims of bad information, and increasingly they are producers of it. They take information from self-interested parties and add to it another layer of self-interest—the desire to sell information."[24]
>
> —Cynthia Crossen, journalist and author of *Tainted Truth: The Manipulation of Fact in America*

research studies and poll results to make it seem as if scientific facts support the ideas they want to spread.

Liberal Bias

The mainstream media have a well-known bias in favor of liberal issues and liberal politicians. Some of the biggest perpetrators of this bias are CNN, the *New York Times*, the *Washington Post*, and NPR—all of whom regularly skew their reporting in favor of liberal causes and attitudes. For example, when President Barrack Obama left office, many journalists repeated a claim that his presidency had been scandal-free. In reality, he had been involved in several controversies, including one in which his administration funded Solyndra, a green energy company that later went bankrupt. "The lack of acknowledgement of actual scandals that were investigated by Congress perfectly encapsulated how the vast majority of the media would not challenge Obama and had a bit too much of a cozy relationship with him,"[26] says Evan Siegfried, a political commentator.

> "Leakers teamed up with liars and liberals at newspapers and television stations on both coasts, all of whom were starving for negative information about the president."[27]
>
> —Jeanine Pirro, Fox News host

This liberal bias works in the other direction as well. Media coverage of Trump's candidacy and presidency has been profoundly negative. According to the Media Research Center, 90 percent of the coverage of Trump on the major news stations ABC, CBS, and NBC during 2017 was negative. From the beginning, the liberal media has desperately wanted to oust the president from office, and it intentionally publishes exaggerated or invented stories in pursuit of this goal. "Leakers teamed up with liars and liberals at newspapers and television stations on both coasts, all of whom were starving for negative information about the president,"[27] writes Jeanine Pirro, a Fox News host. Publications with liberal audiences are more likely to try to please their audience with stories that lament the president's failures and ignore his successes.

Trust in the News Media Is Declining

A Gallup poll conducted yearly asks Americans about their trust in various institutions. Trust in mass media has been declining since polling began. In the 1970s, around 70 percent of Americans had a great deal or fair amount of trust that the mass media reported the news fully, accurately, and fairly. In 2016, that percentage dropped to its lowest-ever level. Though trust climbed back up to 45 percent in 2018, that is still fewer than half of Americans who do not feel they can trust news reports.

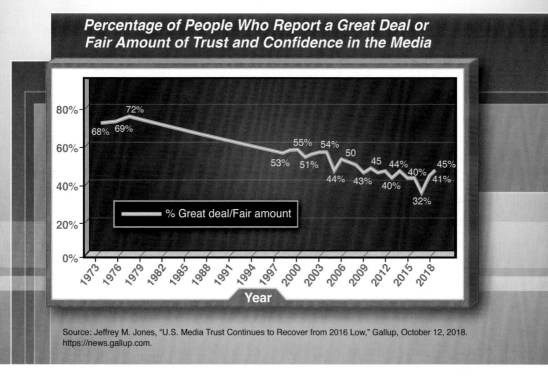

Percentage of People Who Report a Great Deal or Fair Amount of Trust and Confidence in the Media

Source: Jeffrey M. Jones, "U.S. Media Trust Continues to Recover from 2016 Low," Gallup, October 12, 2018. https://news.gallup.com.

Follow the Money

Bias is not the only thing standing in the way of truth. News media organizations are businesses, and to succeed they must attract and retain more customers than their competition. Straightforward, fact-based accounts do not attract as many viewers or prompt as many click-throughs as exciting or sensational stories. People may think they want the truth from media. But their behavior shows that they really want drama, disasters, heroes, and villains. So that is what the majority of mass media provides.

"The system is geared as much to amuse and divert as it is to inform,"[28] Mort Rosenblum, an author, editor, and journalist, wrote in 1993.

The pressure on the news media to produce exciting stories has only increased since then. That is because the Internet and social media allow anyone, anywhere, to produce news. As a result, competition for people's attention is fiercer than ever before. Stories have to stand out in a crowded news feed or no one will click through. This has led to a rise in clickbait, a name for low-quality, sensational content with very little basis in fact. "Digital media companies are caught in the 'crap trap,' mass-producing trashy clickbait so they can claim huge audiences,"[29] says Jim VandeHei, founding editor of *Politico*.

Well-researched, ethically sound news is very time consuming and expensive to produce. And news organizations do not have as much time or money as they once did. Online, anyone can report news instantly. A story becomes old within moments. "Social media has compressed the news cycle from 24 hours to 24 minutes or seconds,"[30] writes Indira A.R. Lakshmanan, an expert in journalism ethics at the Poynter Institute. The news media has to work quickly to keep up. Churning out content at a rapid pace requires cutting corners when it comes to editing and fact-checking.

> "Digital media companies are caught in the 'crap trap,' mass-producing trashy clickbait so they can claim huge audiences."[29]
>
> —Jim VandeHei, founding editor of *Politico*

The Internet has also changed how people pay for their news. Subscriptions to print newspapers and magazines have dropped dramatically as people switch to online news sources, which have traditionally been free to read and supported mainly by advertising revenue. Though paid subscriptions to online newspapers are starting to become popular again, many leading news organizations have suffered during the transition and have had to cut staff. These cutbacks often eliminate positions that help ensure quality and accuracy, such as editors, copy editors, and fact-checkers. In 2017 the *New York Times* announced that it would be laying off a number of editors. The NewsGuild of New York responded that this was "grave news for the state of journalism" and that the eliminated staff members "are the watchdogs that ensure that the truth is told."[31] It is next to impossible for a smaller staff to do the same quality of work as a larger staff.

News organizations gain and retain readers when they report the news their audience wants to hear. This type of news is often biased against certain political ideas. The news media also faces rising pressure to produce news quickly and cheaply. As a result, the media's ability to provide high-quality, ethical journalism has diminished greatly, to the point that the truth no longer seems to matter.

Chapter Three

Should Social Media Companies Censor Fake News?

Social Media Companies Should Control Fake News Content

- Fake news spreads more widely and more quickly than true news on social media.
- Social media must be held to the same standards as traditional media organizations.
- People need help telling the difference between real and fake news on social media.

The Debate at a Glance

Social Media Companies Should Not Censor Their Content

- Censorship of any information, even if the information is false or misleading, threatens the freedom of speech.
- Government directives that aim to stop fake news on social media may have dire consequences for press freedom.
- Social media companies should not be the arbiters of which ideas are worthy and which are not.

Social Media Companies Should Control Fake News Content

"Just as major tech companies have accepted they have a social responsibility to combat piracy online and the illegal sharing of content, they also need to help address the spreading of fake news on social media platforms."

—Damian Collins, UK Parliament member

Quoted in BBC, "Fake News Inquiry by MPs Examines Threat to Democracy," January 30, 2017. www.bbc.com.

Consider these questions as you read:

1. Do you think the fact that fake news spreads faster than real news on social media justifies measures to delete or control fake content? Why or why not?
2. How persuasive is the argument that social media should be held to the same standards as traditional media? Explain your answer.
3. What do you think of the steps social media companies have taken to address the fake news problem? Should they be doing more? Explain.

Editor's note: The discussion that follows presents common arguments made in support of this perspective, reinforced by facts, quotes, and examples taken from various sources.

Social media is the breeding ground for fake news. On Facebook, Twitter, WhatsApp, and other online social platforms, rumors, misinformation, and complete lies often reach more people than facts. What is more, the entities behind false information may be fake themselves. Bots are software programs designed to mimic real people online, often in order to spread fake news. Social media companies must take responsibility for misuse of their platforms and find ways to reduce the impact of fake news.

Spreading Like Wildfire

Fake news is a serious problem on social media. In 2018 officials from Facebook, Twitter, and Google took part in congressional hearings to address fake news and political bias running rampant on their platforms. Though these companies have repeatedly said that they are concerned about the problem, they have not done enough to fix it.

On Twitter, for example, fake stories spread faster and farther than real ones. A team of researchers at the Massachusetts Institute of Technology looked at twelve years of Twitter data and evaluated 126,000 different news items that had been shared on the social media site. The researchers identified each one as either true or false. On average, a false tweet was 70 percent more likely to get a retweet and also reached fifteen hundred people six times faster than a true one. In addition, bots were not to blame for the wide reach of fake stories. Human Twitter users were the ones responsible for spreading the misleading and fake stories.

In a similar study of fake news on Facebook, BuzzFeed reporters analyzed over two thousand posts from just over one thousand pages run by extremely left-wing or right-wing political groups. Most of the content both types of pages shared was mostly true. But mostly false posts were shared many more times than mostly true posts. Alarmingly, people seem to prefer fake news to real news. "If something sounds crazy stupid you wouldn't think it would get that much traction. But those are the [stories] that go massively viral,"[32] says Alex Kasprak, a fact-checker at the website Snopes.

Fake news likely spreads more easily because it has been manufactured to catch and hold people's attention. It usually offers completely new information and provokes strong emotions such as disgust or surprise. And if people believe these false stories, then they may not trust true stories that provide contradictory information. "The real harm from fake news stems from its rapid spread, especially on social media platforms, so that

> "If something sounds crazy stupid you wouldn't think it would get that much traction. But those are the [stories] that go massively viral."[32]
>
> —Alex Kasprak, fact-checker at Snopes

Social Media Companies Must Do More to Prevent the Spread of Fake News

In a poll conducted by YouGov for the *Huffington Post*, Americans made it clear that they want social media companies to take responsibility for the fake news spreading on their platforms. A majority of Americans believe that the rules social media companies currently have in place to limit the spread of false information are not doing enough and that these companies should do more to combat fake news.

Do you think social media outlets like Facebook, Twitter, and YouTube have a responsibility to prevent users from spreading conspiracy theories or false information on their site?

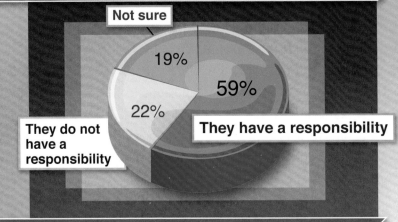

- Not sure — 19%
- They have a responsibility — 59%
- They do not have a responsibility — 22%

In general, do you think the way social media outlets like Facebook, Twitter, and YouTube currently regulate the content posted to their site is:

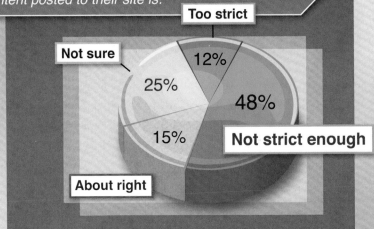

- Too strict — 12%
- Not strict enough — 48%
- About right — 15%
- Not sure — 25%

Source: Ariel Edwards-Levy, "Most People Say Social Media Sites Should Crack Down On Harassment, Fake News: Poll," *Huffington Post*, August 20, 2018. www.huffingtonpost.com.

it undermines trust in all news, corrupts the marketplace of ideas and crowds out real information,"[33] writes Sandeep Gopalan for *The Hill*.

Social Media Is Not Just Social Media Anymore

In newspapers, magazines, and other traditional media, human editors decide which stories deserve the most attention. They also decide which information is worthy of publishing. Social media works very differently. In general, social media technology relies on algorithms that automatically sort content by clicks, shares, likes, and personal relationships. The algorithms know nothing about the truth or intrinsic value of content. And many contributors never edit or fact-check what they share. In this system, the most sensational stories, the ones that spark the most user interaction and reaction, get the most traction. At the same time, high-quality news stories on important but localized subjects have trouble reaching any audience at all. As Emily Bell of the *Guardian* puts it, "Anyone who wants to reach a million people with a poorly produced conspiracy theory video is in luck. If, however, you want to run a well-resourced newsroom covering a town of 200,000 people, that is not going to be sustainable."[34]

> "They can't just say look we're a technology company, we have nothing to do with the content that is appearing on our digital pages."[35]
>
> —Martin Sorrell, founder of WPP

In addition, social media companies —including Google, Facebook, Snapchat, WhatsApp, and Twitter—have become an important source of news for many people. In 2017, 33 percent of people ages eighteen to twenty-four said that social media was their main source of news, according to a report by the Reuters Institute for the Study of Journalism and the University of Oxford. These respondents got their news from social media more often than from online news sites, TV, or newspapers.

When social media becomes a news source, then these platforms must take responsibility for the content they present to their users, just as traditional media do. "They can't just say look we're a technology company, we have nothing to do with the content that is appearing on our digital pages,"[35] said Martin Sorrell of WPP, a company that owns several ad agencies. Though most of the content on social platforms originates with users, social media companies have a lot of control over how that content spreads. When false or harmful material spreads, then these companies must take steps to clean things up. They must take editorial control.

More Must Be Done

Social media companies say that they take the threat fake news poses seriously. Sheryl Sandberg, chief operating officer of Facebook, says, "False news hurts everyone because it makes our community uninformed, it hurts our community, it hurts countries. And we know that people want to see accurate news on Facebook and that's what we want them to see."[36] Facebook and Twitter each regularly weed out bots from their platforms. They will also remove inappropriate material or material that incites violence. But they will not delete a post just because it is false, even if many people find it offensive.

Facebook works with companies that provide fact-checking services to try to limit the spread of fake news. Mark Zuckerberg, chief executive officer of Facebook, explains, "If something is spreading and is rated false by fact checkers, it would lose the vast majority of its distribution in News Feed."[37] Facebook also removed the Trending Topics section of the news feed in 2018. This area was supposed to display interesting news but often wound up spreading fake news instead.

> "False news hurts everyone because it makes our community uninformed, it hurts our community, it hurts countries. And we know that people want to see accurate news on Facebook and that's what we want them to see."[36]
>
> —Sheryl Sandberg, chief operating officer of Facebook

These changes represent small steps in the right direction, but in the end they have not done nearly enough. A 2018 study by researchers at Stanford University and New York University looked at user interactions with fake news on Facebook and Twitter from January 2015 to

July 2018. Though interactions with fake news declined on Facebook after 2016, the study authors stress that the problem has not gone away. "Facebook engagements with fake news sites still average roughly 70 million per month,"[38] the researchers say.

Things are worse on Twitter. Interactions with fake news on this platform have continued to rise. In a 2018 study by the Knight Foundation, researchers found that more than 80 percent of the accounts that spread fake news during the 2016 election were still active. The study reports that "these accounts continue to publish more than a million tweets in a typical day."[39] Twitter clearly has not done enough to weed out sources of harmful fake news.

In addition, many of the approaches social media companies have experimented with to try to combat fake news shift responsibility to their users. For example, in 2018 Facebook announced a plan to ask randomly selected users to rate news sources as trustworthy or untrustworthy. "We decided that having the community determine which sources are broadly trusted would be most objective,"[40] says Zuckerberg. Many criticized the plan. Fake news outlets already make fake accounts to artificially promote their content. They would likely find ways to artificially rate themselves as trustworthy. A move such as this demonstrates how reluctant social media companies are to spend time and money eradicating the fake news circulating on their platforms.

There are many steps Twitter and other social media companies could and should take to promote accurate, objective news. For example, lists exist of websites known to produce reliable or fake content. Facebook could use these lists to alert a user when he or she is about to share something that may be fake. Alberto Alemanno, founder of the EU Public Interest Clinic, says, "We should be thinking about changing the environment in which readers act, and empowering them: displaying related, fact-checked articles next to disputed stories; apps allowing users to check for veracity; certification systems."[41] Facebook and other social media giants must continue to invest in improving the quality of the news their users encounter.

Social Media Companies Should Not Censor Their Content

"Free speech should not be sacrificed in an attempt to combat fake news."

—Sandeep Gopalan, law professor at Deakin University

Sandeep Gopalan, "Free Speech Cannot Be Sacrificed to Strike Fake News," *The Hill* (Washington, DC), April 6, 2018. https://thehill.com.

Consider these questions as you read:

1. How important is free and open discourse in a democracy? Why?
2. How would you draw the line between critical speech and hate speech, and at what point should the right to free speech no longer be protected?
3. Do you think laws against fake news on social media are ever justified? Why or why not?

Editor's note: The discussion that follows presents common arguments made in support of this perspective, reinforced by facts, quotes, and examples taken from various sources.

Removing links to fake content from social media or banning bots sounds like an honorable mission. Weeding out falsehoods and punishing those who spread them may seem like the best way to have honest, open discussions as a society. But there is a huge problem with this idea: Someone has to decide which content is true and which is false. The person, company, or government making that decision wields power over the truth and may use this power unfairly or unwisely. In the end, any policing of information amounts to censorship and threatens the freedom of speech.

Social Media Platforms Censor Valid Points of View

Requiring social media companies to control content endangers the free expression of ideas. A 2018 Pew Research Center survey found that the majority of Americans believe social media companies actively and intentionally censor valid viewpoints on their platforms. Republicans especially believe that social media is politically biased in favor of liberal views. And among all Americans, 72 percent say that it is likely that these companies censor points of view they do not agree with. In a free society, this type of censorship should not occur.

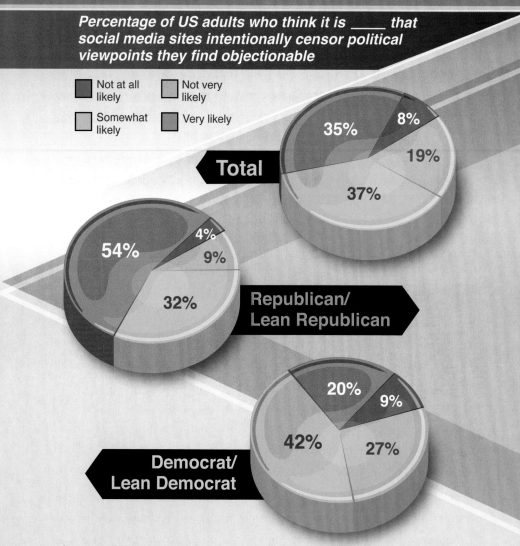

Percentage of US adults who think it is _____ that social media sites intentionally censor political viewpoints they find objectionable

Not at all likely
Not very likely
Somewhat likely
Very likely

Total
35%
8%
19%
37%

Republican/ Lean Republican
54%
4%
9%
32%

Democrat/ Lean Democrat
20%
9%
42%
27%

Source: Aaron Smith, "Public Attitudes Towards Technology Companies," Pew Research Center, June 28, 2018. http://assets.pewresearch.org.

A Threat to Free Speech

Free speech is a fundamental part of American culture and of democracy in general. Amnesty International defines free speech as the right to share "information and ideas of all kinds, by any means."[42] In other words, people should be free to take a stand and share their ideas. And they should have this freedom even if those ideas are distasteful, inaccurate, or harshly critical. Speech should only be restricted or punished if it puts others at risk of discrimination or violence. Fake news, even if it is completely fabricated, should not be silenced unless it also qualifies as hate speech. Freedom of the press is an essential component of free speech because the press is what allows ideas to spread to a wide audience. Today the press includes every single person on social media. All of these voices should have the freedom to speak, even if what they have to say is false, unkind, or scandalous. At the same time, members of the public always have a choice of what to read or watch. So they are able to choose the best or most reliable sources of information.

With the advent of social media and the Internet, though, many experts have worried that people are no longer capable of sorting through the deluge of information and discerning which sources are honest and which are untrustworthy. Some argue that people now need protection from bad information and that social media companies such as Facebook, Twitter, Instagram, WhatsApp, and others have a responsibility to remove fake news from their platforms. Some lament the days when people could rely on vetted news from professional journalists via newspaper articles and television broadcasts. The Internet has been viewed as "a cauldron of lies and falsehoods,"[43] writes Matthew Fraser of the American University of Paris. However, expecting social media companies to control fake news is asking for trouble. Any top-down attempt to remove or restrict fake news will threaten free speech.

Misguided Attempts to Regulate

When a society decides that social media must address the fake news problem, the most straightforward way to make sure a change happens is through new laws that regulate how these companies do business. Social media companies must comply or risk losing their ability to reach customers in that country. Unfortunately, these types of laws often put a society on a slippery slope toward more sweeping rules that may restrict free speech.

For example, in 2018 France passed a law that allows judges to order the removal of fake news from the Internet during political campaigns. Sweden, Ireland, and the Czech Republic are considering similar laws. Critics point out that because "fake news" has such a loose definition, a government could use this type of law to remove any information. In 2018 French politician Julien Rochedy said on Twitter, "The French state finally has a monopoly on truth and mass diffusion. It can legally censor anything it doesn't like."[44] In these countries, social media companies may soon be forced to take down controversial but legitimate speech to prevent breaking the law. "In a democratic society, surely the arbiter of truth and falsehood must never be the state,"[45] writes Fraser. In fact, in the United States a government effort to regulate information on social media would likely violate the First Amendment.

> "In a democratic society, surely the arbiter of truth and falsehood must never be the state."[45]
>
> —Matthew Fraser of the American University of Paris

It may seem safer to make social media companies responsible for policing fake news on their own. These private companies are actually not subject to the First Amendment. In the United States they technically have the freedom to set whatever rules they want for discourse on their platforms. And they dislike being seen as purveyors of fake news. But any attempts to control fake accounts and fake content are always controversial. "A move to force tech companies to decide what is posted online could give significant powers to a few private companies like Twitter and Facebook,"[46] write Mark Scott and Janosch Delcker for *Politico*. These corporations could end up with the same power over truth as a dictatorship that keeps a firm grip on its media. Both Facebook and Twitter have publicly stated that they do not want to tightly control their content. "We definitely don't want to be the arbiter of the truth,"[47] said Sheryl Sandberg in 2017. In 2018 the Twitter Safety account tweeted,

"We welcome everyone to express themselves on our service. Sometimes these expressions may be offensive, controversial, and/or bigoted."[48]

Caught in a Purge

Despite these public positions, Facebook and Twitter have each taken measures to remove fake accounts and news from their sites. They have each purged what they say are bots and other problematic accounts. They say they do this to protect the integrity of their services. "Inauthentic accounts, spam, and malicious automation disrupt everyone's experience on Twitter, and we will never be done with our efforts to identify and prevent attempts to manipulate conversations on our platform,"[49] wrote Twitter executives Yoel Roth and Del Harvey in 2018. In May and June 2018 alone, the company suspended 70 million accounts. Many prominent figures on Twitter lost thousands of followers. Conservatives and right-wing activists claimed they were unfairly targeted in the purge. "I've definitely been locked out and unfairly targeted because I'm a Trump supporter who also tweets out Bible verses,"[50] complained one Twitter user who wished to remain anonymous.

Also in 2018, Facebook removed eight hundred political pages and accounts for breaking rules against spam and "inauthentic" behavior. Facebook said the pages and accounts were either fake or spamming people with political content that was not legitimate in order to drive traffic to their websites. Marc Belisle once worked for Reverb Press, a liberal media outlet that was one of the affected pages. "Facebook is completely unqualified to determine what kinds of political discussion are legitimate," he says. "And this goes for sites across the political spectrum, including the many conservative pages caught up in the latest purge: I disagree with their arguments, but I believe absolutely in their right to reach their audience on Facebook."[51]

> "A move to force tech companies to decide what is posted online could give significant powers to a few private companies like Twitter and Facebook."[46]
>
> —Mark Scott and Janosch Delcker, journalists at *Politico*

> "Drawing the line between 'real' and 'inauthentic' views is a difficult enterprise that could put everything from important political parody to genuine but outlandish views on the chopping block."[52]
>
> —Vera Eidelman of the American Civil Liberties Union

Liberals and conservatives seem to agree on at least one thing: Social media companies should not be responsible for deciding which ideas are worthy and which are not. Their purges will never eliminate all fake content and will occasionally accidentally censor real content. "Drawing the line between 'real' and 'inauthentic' views is a difficult enterprise that could put everything from important political parody to genuine but outlandish views on the chopping block,"[52] says Vera Eidelman of the American Civil Liberties Union. Ideally, the ultimate authority over which news to distribute, consume, and trust should remain where it has always been in a democratic society: with the people. Governments and companies should never take it upon themselves to censor the media.

Chapter Four

Can People Resist the Influence of Fake News?

People Can Learn to Resist the Influence of Fake News

- Members of the public must resist fake news because objective truth is at the heart of scientific understanding.
- Schools can teach kids information literacy so they can recognize fake news.
- Most people care about the truth and seek out factual reporting.

The Debate at a Glance

People Cannot Resist the Influence of Fake News

- Stories that appeal to emotions or political ideology influence people much more than facts ever will.
- Filter bubbles and echo chambers divide people and make them even more likely to resist facts.
- In a post-truth world, the idea of objective truth has been replaced with alternative facts.

People Can Learn to Resist the Influence of Fake News

"I have a responsibility as an individual to be more self-aware and a better consumer of information."

—Katie Harper, graduate student in library and information science

Quoted in University of Washington, "Understanding Fake News and Misinformation," May 29, 2018. www.washington.edu.

Consider these questions as you read:

1. How strong is the argument that media literacy can counter the effects of fake news? Explain your answer.
2. What do you conclude from the fact that students are easily fooled by fake news yet care about the truth?
3. Do you think a survey asking people whether they check the accuracy of news stories is a reliable indicator of how people actually behave? Why or why not?

Editor's note: The discussion that follows presents common arguments made in support of this perspective, reinforced by facts, quotes, and examples taken from various sources.

No matter what steps governments and social media companies take to tackle the problem of fake news, it is not going to go away anytime soon. Disinformation, misinformation, and propaganda have always existed and will likely exist far into the future. But people have a choice. Instead of falling for fake news, they can fight it.

Taking Personal Responsibility

Education in media literacy helps people separate facts from lies, opinions, and misrepresentations. "We don't need new policies and tools from tech companies to identify sketchy content on the web," says Bill Ferriter, a teacher in North Carolina. "Instead we need to develop citizens who take careful steps to verify that the information they are reading anywhere on the web is reliable."[53] People must also understand the scientific method, since this is the best way to arrive at objective truth about the world. All individuals must take personal responsibility for the news they consume and share and for the facts they believe. This is the most effective way for society to resist the influence of false and misleading information.

Objective, critical thinkers gather evidence before deciding what to believe. If new evidence counters their beliefs, they discard those beliefs and start over. This approach is at the heart of scientific understanding. It has led to a shared set of facts about the world that allow researchers to make progress in science, engineering, medicine, and other important fields.

> "We need to develop citizens who take careful steps to verify that the information they are reading anywhere on the web is reliable."[53]
>
> —Bill Ferriter, teacher in North Carolina

In the scientific method, a person performs experiments and collects evidence to check whether the theory about the world is valid. Other scientists repeat these experiments. It does not matter what the scientific community wants to be true. Evidence from the world reveals the actual truth. "Scientists . . . pursue evidence based solutions, regardless of TV ratings, circulation numbers or social media 'likes,'"[54] says Maryanne Reed of West Virginia University. She goes on to say that journalists should try a similar approach to their craft. They should let facts and evidence lead them to a conclusion.

Teaching Media Literacy

Consumers of news usually do not have the time or resources to go out and collect evidence. They may only have a few seconds to decide whether to believe or disbelieve information. "The speed at which we are being bombarded with stories claiming to be news has created a world in which a person who is unable to differentiate between true and untrue stories is functionally illiterate,"[55] writes Carli V. Lowe for *American Libraries* magazine.

Students Value Truthful News Reporting

Students understand the importance of seeking out factual, accurate reporting and believe that it is not that difficult to avoid fake news. In a survey of more than fifty-five hundred students at eleven different US colleges and universities, the Knight Foundation found that most agreed that news should be factual or objective and that this is important in a democracy. A much smaller percentage of students felt it was difficult to identify fake news.

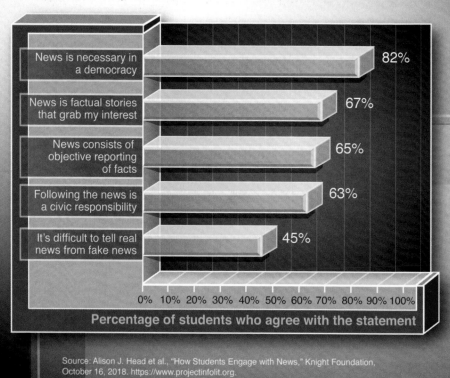

News is necessary in a democracy — 82%

News is factual stories that grab my interest — 67%

News consists of objective reporting of facts — 65%

Following the news is a civic responsibility — 63%

It's difficult to tell real news from fake news — 45%

0% 10% 20% 30% 40% 50% 60% 70% 80% 90% 100%

Percentage of students who agree with the statement

Source: Alison J. Head et al., "How Students Engage with News," Knight Foundation, October 16, 2018. https://www.projectinfolit.org.

The best solution to this problem is media literacy education. A media literate person approaches videos, photographs, articles, tweets, and all other forms of media with a critical, skeptical eye. To evaluate the content, he or she traces it back to an original source, looks for independent confirmation from other sources, and keeps an eye out for signs of bias or a lack of context that may lead to misunderstanding. He or she also understands how to seek out credible information and produce credible content. "The power of media literacy is its ability to inspire independent thinking and foster critical analysis,"[56] says the Center for Media Literacy. It is essential that this training reach as many people as possible.

Many schools and organizations offer classes, workshops, and other resources that teach media literacy skills. A number of US states—including California, Connecticut, and Washington—have passed laws related to media literacy education. The California law requires that the state provide students and teachers with media literacy resources. "We already require critical thinking skills in our schools. By giving students the proper training to analyze the media they consume, we can empower them to make informed decisions,"[57] says Bill Dodd, the California state senator who introduced the law.

But education in these skills is not widespread enough. Researchers at Stanford University have assessed the media literacy of students in middle school, high school, and college. Most of the students could not identify credible information. "When it comes to evaluating information that flows through social media channels, they are easily duped,"[58] say the researchers. For example, middle school students had to differentiate the advertisements from the real news stories on a website. Eighty percent of them believed that a piece marked sponsored content (a type of advertisement) was a real news story. College students saw a tweet and had to evaluate whether it was a good source of data. Less than a third of them pointed out that a political activist group had created the tweet, so it was likely biased.

> "We already require critical thinking skills in our schools. By giving students the proper training to analyze the media they consume, we can empower them to make informed decisions."[57]
>
> —Bill Dodd, California state senator

In many other similar exercises, the majority of students performed poorly. They rarely made an effort to investigate information. Sam Wineburg, who led the research, says, "We really can't blame young people because we've never taught them to do otherwise."[59] Schools have to do more to prepare kids for a world polluted with fake news.

People Want the Facts

Finding credible news online takes time and effort. However, research has shown that many people are willing to take steps to avoid biased and fake information. A 2017 survey from Michigan State University asked Internet users in seven different countries how they use online searches to learn about politics. Fifty percent of the respondents say they check the accuracy of news stories often or very often, and only 5 percent say they never do. Checking accuracy reveals a commitment to thinking independently about an event or idea and is a sign of media literacy. William H. Dutton, who led the research, says, "Internet users generally rely on a diverse array of sources for political information. And they display a healthy skepticism, leading them to question information and check facts."[60]

Young people care about the truth as well. A 2018 survey by the Knight Foundation and Project Information Literacy found that 82 percent of college students agreed that news is necessary in a democracy, and about two-thirds thought that news consisted of objective reporting of facts. However, fear of fake news made it difficult for them to trust any news. Only 14 percent felt very confident that they could identify fake news. One student says, "It is really hard to know what is real in today's society; there are a lot of news sources and it is difficult to trust any of them."[61] Another says, "No news source is entirely credible but I think you can piece it together if you pull from enough different news sources."[62]

Though many people use social media as a news source, they generally understand that opinionated, biased, and sensational stories are often more prominent on these platforms than factual stories. In a 2018 study, the Pew Research Center found that about two-thirds of adults in the United States get news on social media. At the same time, around two-thirds of adults expect news on social media to be largely inaccurate. In fact, inaccuracy was the issue that most bothered people about getting news on social media. It was even more concerning than political bias or bad behavior of other users.

All of these survey results support the idea that people know they should be critical and skeptical of the news they read, especially on social media. And many people are willing to work to get to the facts. With a concerted effort and better training in media literacy and science, people can and will resist the effects of fake news.

People Cannot Resist the Influence of Fake News

"Facts rarely matter to an ideologue who has made up his or her mind."

—Jason Altmire, writer for *The Hill*

Jason Altmire, "The Importance of Fact-Checking in a Post-truth World," *The Hill* (Washington, DC), September 8, 2018. https://thehill.com.

Consider these questions as you read:

1. How convincing is the argument that emotions rule human decision-making? Explain.
2. Why do you think social media makes it easy for people to isolate themselves into echo chambers?
3. How can people communicate effectively in a post-truth world?

Editor's note: The discussion that follows presents common arguments made in support of this perspective, reinforced by facts, quotes, and examples taken from various sources.

People like to believe that they are smart and rational. They learn in school about the scientific method, evidence-based conclusions, and critical thinking. Many students also learn media literacy skills. While training like this can help a person resist some fake news, it will never be entirely effective. Humans are naturally irrational and emotional thinkers. Fake or misleading content that appeals to emotion and entrenched values will always fool people, no matter how smart they are.

Feelings vs. Facts

Many people think that if you provide people with facts, they will follow those facts to the correct conclusion. But especially when emotions and values are involved, that is not what happens. Emotions prevail in decision-making. Politicians and advertisers have long understood that emotional content is much more persuasive than facts and logic. That is why ads are filled with images, music, and stories meant to provoke anger, outrage, disgust, and other strong emotions. Fake news creators also understand the power of emotion. "We're constantly trying to tune into feelings that we think that people already have or want to have,"[63] says the owner of a prominent fake news website.

The problem with expecting people to resist fake news is that people are not actually motivated by truth. They may think they are, but in reality they are motivated to protect their core values and beliefs. "Our decision-making, while feeling evidence-based to us, is really value-based," writes Tamar Haspel in the *Washington Post*. "We're driven by our tribes, our affiliations and our instincts, and we see evidence through that prism. Confirmation bias rules the human psyche."[64] Confirmation bias means paying close attention to facts that support an existing belief while ignoring facts that challenge that belief.

In some cases, using facts to try to convince someone that an existing belief is wrong may cause a person to strengthen his or her commitment to the original, incorrect belief. Researchers at Dartmouth College named this the backfire effect. They looked at what happens when people who are concerned about getting a flu shot read facts about how the shot does not cause the flu. The facts actually made some people less willing to get the shot. The fact is, people stubbornly resist changing their views. Despite overwhelming scientific evidence to the contrary, some people persist in believing that climate change is not real or that vaccinations cause autism.

> "Our decision-making, while feeling evidence-based to us, is really value-based. We're driven by our tribes, our affiliations and our instincts, and we see evidence through that prism. Confirmation bias rules the human psyche."[64]
>
> —Tamar Haspel, writer for the *Washington Post*

The Ability to Detect Fake News Is Declining

Many young professionals who have grown up with digital technology believe they think critically about the information they consume. Surveys conducted in 2017 and 2018 by the education company MindEdge show this to be inaccurate. In 2018, 59 percent of the survey respondents were very confident in their critical-thinking ability, but 52 percent of them failed a nine-question quiz testing their ability to spot false information. That was an increase in failures over the previous year. The number of respondents who managed to answer eight to nine questions correctly also dropped in 2018.

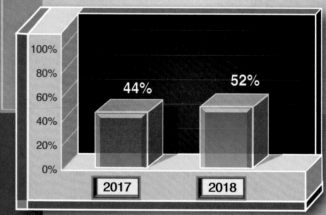

Percentage of respondents that flunked the critical-thinking quiz:

	2017	2018
	44%	52%

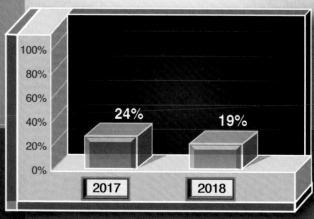

Percentage of respondents that answered eight to nine questions correctly:

	2017	2018
	24%	19%

Filter Bubbles

The Internet makes it easier than ever before for groups of people to cling to certain beliefs. That is because the algorithms powering social media and search engines filter information for people using their preferences and previous behavior. Every tap, share, or like informs the algorithm about a user's preferences and makes it more likely for the user to encounter certain types of content and less likely to see other types. In addition, people curate their own information by choosing who to follow or unfollow on social media and by subscribing to news and updates from certain groups and media organizations.

Eli Pariser, an activist and author, came up with the term *filter bubble* for this type of personalized information. It is a problem because the bubble "fundamentally alters the way we encounter ideas and information,"[65] he says. Filter bubbles hide information, opinions, and facts that do not align with a person's existing experience and perspective. This may create so-called echo chambers of people who all share common values. These groups do not get exposed to people who think differently, which may foster groupthink, a situation in which individuals simply agree with a group instead of making independent decisions. Pariser says, "Democracy requires citizens to see things from one another's point of view, but instead we're more and more enclosed in our own bubbles. Democracy requires a reliance on shared facts; instead we're being offered parallel but separate universes."[66]

> "Democracy requires citizens to see things from one another's point of view, but instead we're more and more enclosed in our own bubbles. Democracy requires a reliance on shared facts; instead we're being offered parallel but separate universes."[66]
>
> —Eli Pariser, activist and author

Echo Chambers

Research has found evidence that echo chambers are common on social media. In a 2017 study published in *PNAS*, researchers found that Facebook users around the world tend to access a limited set of pages.

One of the researchers, Walter Quattrociocchi of the IMT School for Advanced Studies in Italy, says, "People fall into groups where they reinforce their views and ignore dissenting views."[67] So even though the Internet is home to an astonishing variety of perspectives and ideas, most people never see all these ideas. They stay in their comfort zones, among like-minded people.

In an echo chamber, the group's agreement and support makes members even more sure that they are right and justified in their beliefs. This can drive people away from reasonable, balanced thinking about an issue and toward extremist views. In one study, researchers put together small groups of people with similar political views to discuss controversial topics for fifteen minutes. They asked participants for their anonymous opinions on the topics before and after the discussion. Afterward, people's opinions became more extreme. "Deliberation among like-minded people can increase extremism, intensify polarization, and also squelch internal disagreement,"[68] writes Cass Sunstein, one of the researchers.

> "People fall into groups where they reinforce their views and ignore dissenting views."[67]
>
> —Walter Quattrociocchi, researcher at the IMT School for Advanced Studies

On social media, participating in discussions with groups of like-minded people also likely fortifies beliefs—whether those beliefs are true or not. This means that if a group accepts fake news as real or dismisses real news as fake, most members of the group will go along with the consensus. And on social media, some members of a group may not even be human. They could be bots planted to artificially make it seem as if a lot of people support a certain idea. The bots could get real people to go along with ideas they may not otherwise decide to support. "Bots are providing the online crowds that are providing legitimacy,"[69] says Jonathan Albright, a professor at Elon University.

A Post-truth World

Most people believe that they value the truth. They may think that they make objective, logical decisions. But when it comes down to it, loyalty to a community and adherence to deeply held beliefs and values will almost always overwhelm factual evidence. "We communicate cynically and gullibly—we believe nothing the other side says and everything our side says,"[70] writes Jennifer Mercieca for Zócalo Public Square.

At the same time, identifying factual information is harder than ever before. Search engines and social media throw all types of information together into one bucket. On Facebook and Twitter, links to articles from serious news organizations that took a team of people months to research and write pop up alongside links to rants and opinions that one person spent a few hours thinking about. Real news, advertisements, jokes, political propaganda, and entirely fake stories jumble together in search results. Media that were once accepted as accurate records of events—such as photographs, videos, and audio recordings—can now be doctored or entirely fabricated to show an invented reality. The result is that people around the world are confused about whom and what to trust. Some scholars have started to call the time we are living in the post-truth era. It is a time when society cannot agree on a common reality, and feelings have more impact on public opinion than facts or evidence. People just cannot resist the influence of fake news.

However, all is not lost. The human tendencies of emotional thinking and group loyalty can be harnessed for good. Instead of hurling unwanted and unconvincing facts at each other, people should be seeking to understand the emotions underlying their opponents' positions. Ari Brown, a pediatrician in Texas, has found that the best way to communicate with parents who are reluctant to vaccinate is through personal connections. She tells the parents of her patients that she is a mom and vaccinates her own kids. "At the end of the day, the science is not going to convince them. What convinces them is the emotion,"[71] says Brown. In a post-truth world, people have to move beyond facts and lies. They have to actively listen to each other and empathize with each other in order to reach common understanding.

Source Notes

Overview: Fake News

1. Quoted in Janna Anderson and Lee Rainie, "The Future of Truth and Misinformation Online," Pew Research Center, October 19, 2017. www.pewinternet.org.
2. Craig Silverman, "I Helped Popularize the Term 'Fake News' and Now I Cringe Every Time I Hear It," BuzzFeed News, December 31, 2017. www.buzzfeednews.com.
3. Quoted in Emma Jane Kirby, "The City Getting Rich from Fake News," BBC, December 5, 2016. www.bbc.com.
4. Quoted in Tamara Keith, "President Trump's Description of What's 'Fake' Is Expanding," NPR, September 2, 2018. www.npr.org.
5. Donald Trump (@realDonaldTrump), "The media has been speculating that I fired Rex Tillerson or that he would be leaving soon—FAKE NEWS!," Twitter, December 1, 2017. https://twitter.com.

Chapter One: Does Fake News Pose a Serious Threat?

6. Quoted in Anisa Sudebar, "The Godfather of Fake News," BBC, November 27, 2018. www.bbc.co.uk.
7. Claire McCarthy, "Immunization in the Era of Fake News—What Do Pediatricians Need to Do?," *AAP Voices* (blog), American Academy of Pediatrics, April 24, 2017. www.aap.org.
8. Richard Gunther, Paul A. Beck, and Erik C. Nisbet, "Fake News Did Have a Significant Impact on the Vote in the 2016 Election," Ohio State University. https://cpb-us-w2.wpmucdn.com.
9. Quoted in Radio Free Europe/Radio Liberty, "U.K. PM Says Russia Will Not Succeed in 'Sowing Discord in West,'" November 15, 2017. www.rferl.org.
10. Quoted in Judy Woodruff, "What's Happened to the Truth Under President Trump?," *PBS NewsHour*, July 25, 2018. www.pbs.org.
11. Quoted in Woodruff, "What's Happened to the Truth Under President Trump?"

12. Donald A. Barclay, *Fake News, Propaganda, and Plain Old Lies*. Lanham, MD: Rowman & Littlefield, 2018, p. 45.

13. Vaughan Bell, "Don't Touch That Dial!," *Slate*, February 15, 2010. https://slate.com.

14. Matthew Fraser, "Debate: The Legal Fight Against 'Fake News' Must Not Veer into Censorship," Conversation, June 11, 2018. https://theconversation.com.

15. Quoted in Benedict Carey, "'Fake News': Wide Reach but Little Impact, Study Suggests," *New York Times*, January 2, 2018. www.nytimes.com.

16. Duncan J. Watts and David M. Rothschild, "Don't Blame the Election on Fake News. Blame It on the Media," *Columbia Journalism Review*, December 5, 2017. www.cjr.org.

Chapter Two: Does the News Media Tell the Truth?

17. Editorial Board, "Our View: The Best Defense Against Tyranny Is a Free and Independent Press," *Portland (ME) Press Herald*, August 16, 2018. www.pressherald.com.

18. Society of Professional Journalists, "SPJ Code of Ethics," September 6, 2014. www.spj.org.

19. Quoted in Rachel McAthy, "Made a Mistake? Advice for Journalists on Online Corrections," Journalism.co.uk, January 21, 2013. www.journalism.co.uk.

20. Quoted in McAthy, "Made a Mistake?"

21. Quoted in William P. Davis, "'Enemy of the People': Trump Breaks Out This Phrase During Moments of Peak Criticism," *New York Times*, July 19, 2018. www.nytimes.com.

22. Susan Shultz, "Editorial: There Is Nothing More Patriotic or American than a Free Press," *Darien (CT) Times*, August 16, 2018. www.darientimes.com.

23. Katharine Viner, "A Mission for Journalism in a Time of Crisis," *Guardian* (Manchester), November 16, 2017. www.theguardian.com.

24. Quoted in Peter Vanderwicken, "Why the News Is Not the Truth," *Harvard Business Review*, May–June 1995. https://hbr.org.

25. Vanderwicken, "Why the News Is Not the Truth."

26. Evan Siegfried, "Media Bias Against Conservatives Is Real, and Part of the Reason No One Trusts the News Now," *NBC News*, July 29, 2018. www.nbcnews.com.

27. Jeanine Pirro, *Liars, Leakers, and Liberals*. New York: Center Street, 2018, p. 25.

28. Quoted in Vanderwicken, "Why the News Is Not the Truth."

29. Jim VandeHei, "Escaping the Digital Media 'Crap Trap,'" *Information*, April 19, 2016. www.theinformation.com.

30. Indira A.R. Lakshmanan, "*New York Times* Editing Cuts Mean Doing More with Less. Will Credibility Suffer?," Poynter Institute, June 2, 2017. www.poynter.org.

31. Quoted in Lakshmanan, "*New York Times* Editing Cuts Mean Doing More with Less."

Chapter Three: Should Social Media Companies Censor Fake News?

32. Quoted in Katie Langin, "Fake News Spreads Faster than True News on Twitter—Thanks to People, Not Bots," *Science*, March 8, 2018. www.sciencemag.org.

33. Sandeep Gopalan, "Free Speech Cannot Be Sacrificed to Strike Fake News," *The Hill* (Washington, DC), April 6, 2018. https://thehill.com.

34. Emily Bell, "Technology Company? Publisher? The Lines Can No Longer Be Blurred," *Guardian* (Manchester), April 2, 2017. www.theguardian.com.

35. Quoted in Geoff Cutmore, "Facebook, Google Need to 'Step Up' Control of Their Platforms, Says WPP's Martin Sorrell," CNBC, March 20, 2017. www.cnbc.com.

36. Quoted in Arjun Kharpal, "Facebook Doesn't Want to Be the 'Arbiter of the Truth,' Top Exec Sheryl Sandberg Says, amid Fake News Criticism," CNBC, April 24, 2017. www.cnbc.com.

37. Quoted in Kara Swisher, "Mark Zuckerberg Clarifies: 'I Personally Find Holocaust Denial Deeply Offensive, and I Absolutely Didn't Intend to Defend the Intent of People Who Deny That,'" Recode, July 18, 2018. www.recode.net.

38. Hunt Allcott et al., "Trends in the Diffusion of Misinformation on Social Media," Stanford University, October 2018. http://web.stanford.edu.

39. Knight Foundation, "Disinformation, 'Fake News,' and Influence Campaigns on Twitter," October 4, 2018. www.knightfoundation.org.

40. Quoted in Rob Price, "Facebook's Survey to Assess the Trustworthiness of News Is Only 2 Questions Long—but Says That's Not an Issue," *Business Insider*, January 23, 2018. www.businessinsider.com.

41. Quoted in Jon Henley, "Global Crackdown on Fake News Raises Censorship Concerns," *Guardian* (Manchester), April 24, 2018. www.theguardian.com.

42. Amnesty International, "What Is Freedom of Speech?," August 14, 2018. www.amnesty.org.uk.

43. Fraser, "Debate."

44. Quoted in Michael-Ross Fiorentino, "France Passes Controversial 'Fake News' Law," Euronews, November 22, 2018. www.euronews.com.

45. Fraser, "Debate."

46. Mark Scott and Janosch Delcker, "Free Speech vs. Censorship in Germany," *Politico*, January 4, 2018. www.politico.eu.

47. Quoted in Kharpal, "Facebook Doesn't Want to Be the 'Arbiter of the Truth,' Top Exec Sheryl Sandberg Says, amid Fake News Criticism."

48. Quoted in Karissa Bell, "Twitter Is Basically OK with Harassment, Just Don't @ Anyone," Mashable, August 7, 2018. https://mashable.com.

49. Yoel Roth and Del Harvey, "How Twitter Is Fighting Spam and Malicious Automation," Twitter, June 26, 2018. https://blog.twitter.com.

50. Quoted in Matt Novak, "Conservative Twitter Users Lose Thousands of Followers, Mass Purge of Bots Suspected [Updated]," Gizmodo, February 21, 2018. https://gizmodo.com.

51. Marc Belisle, "Everything I Wrote Was True and Accurate. So Why Did Facebook Purge My Work?," BuzzFeed News, October 17, 2018. www.buzzfeednews.com.

52. Quoted in Dan Tynan, "Facebook Accused of Censorship After Hundreds of US Political Pages Purged," *Guardian* (Manchester), October 16, 2018. www.theguardian.com.

Chapter Four: Can People Resist the Influence of Fake News?

53. Quoted in Tim Walker, "Who Stands Between Fake News and Students? Educators," *NEA Today*, December 16, 2016. http://nea today.org.

54. Quoted in Daniel Klyn et al., "'Is Truth Overrated?' What the Experts Say," Conversation, September 8, 2017. https://theconversa tion.com.

55. Carli V. Lowe, "Fake News or Free Speech: Is There a Right to Be Misinformed?," *American Libraries*, June 25, 2018. https://american librariesmagazine.org.

56. Center for Media Literacy, "Empowerment Through Education." www.medialit.org.

57. Quoted in Marissa Melton, "California Joins Other States in Passing New Media Literacy Law," Voice of America, September 23, 2018. www.voanews.com.

58. Quoted in Daniel Funke, "Study: Fake News Is Making College Students Question All News," Poynter Institute, October 16, 2018. www.poynter.org.

59. Quoted in Camila Domonoske, "Students Have 'Dismaying' Inability to Tell Fake News from Real, Study Finds," NPR, November 23, 2016. www.npr.org.

60. William H. Dutton, "Fake News, Echo Chambers and Filter Bubbles: Underresearched and Overhyped," Conversation, May 5, 2017. https://theconversation.com.

61. Quoted in Alison J. Head et al., "How Students Engage with News," Knight Foundation, October 16, 2018. www.knightfoundation.org.

62. Quoted in Head et al., "How Students Engage with News."

63. Quoted in BBC, "The Rise and Rise of Fake News," November 6, 2016. www.bbc.com.

64. Tamar Haspel, "The Cure for Partisanship in Food Debates: Start Listening," *Washington Post*, December 21, 2018. www.washington post.com.

65. Quoted in *Mental Models* (blog), Farnam Street, "How Filter Bubbles Distort Reality: Everything You Need to Know," 2017. https://fs.blog/2017/07/filter-bubbles/.

66. Quoted in *Mental Models* (blog), "How Filter Bubbles Distort Reality."

67. Quoted in Rebecca Ruiz, "Echo Chambers on Facebook Aren't the Media's Fault. It's Yours," Mashable, March 6, 2017. https://mash able.com.

68. Cass Sunstein, "Deliberation Day and Political Extremism," University of Chicago Law School, February 2, 2006. https://uchicagolaw .typepad.com.

69. Quoted in Darrell M. West, "How to Combat Fake News and Disinformation," Brookings Institution, December 18, 2017. www.brook ings.edu.

70. Jennifer Mercieca, "Preaching Civility Won't Save American Democracy," Zócalo Public Square, December 18, 2018. www.zocalopublic square.org.

71. Quoted in NBC News, "Pro-vaccine Messages Actually Backfire, Study Finds," March 3, 2014. www.nbcnews.com.

Fake News Facts

Telling Truth from Lies

- A 2017 survey by Northwest Arkansas Community College found that 58 percent of Americans believe the mainstream media distribute fake news sometimes or most of the time.
- A 2016 survey by the Pew Research Center found that 64 percent of Americans believe fake news has caused a great deal of confusion about the basic facts of current events.
- In a 2018 Pew Research Center survey, only one-quarter of Americans could correctly identify ten statements as either fact or opinion.
- In a 2016 study, researchers at Stanford University found that more than 80 percent of high school students were fooled by a misleading photograph.
- Deep fakes are hoax videos or sound bites that use digital processing tricks to show a real person doing or saying something that the person never actually did or said.

Fake News in US Politics

- Real news websites had forty times more visitors on average than fake news websites during 2016, according to a study published in *New Media & Society*.
- In the months leading up to the 2016 election, the top twenty fake news stories on Facebook had more engagement (likes, shares, and comments) than the top twenty real news stories, according to an analysis by BuzzFeed.
- A single fake story, claiming President Obama had banned the Pledge of Allegiance in schools, had 2.2 million engagements on Facebook, according to data from BuzzSumo.
- A 2016 survey by Ipsos Public Affairs found that US adults believed election-related fake news headlines 75 percent of the time.

- Around 80 percent of fake news stories spread leading up to the 2016 election supported Donald Trump, according to a study published in the *Journal of Economic Perspectives.*
- As of 2018, Trump had used the term *fake news* 225 times on Twitter, according to *Politico.*

Fake News in the World

- As of 2016, some fake news creators made from $5,000 to $10,000 per month in online ad revenue, according to the *Washington Post.*
- In 2018 around 200 million people in India shared a fake video and warning about kidnappers on WhatsApp, leading to the deaths of at least two dozen innocent people.
- In 2018 France passed a law that allows judges to order the removal of fake news during an election.
- As of 2018, there were 156 active fact-checking projects and organizations around the world, according to the Duke Reporters' Lab.

Fake News on Social Media

- A Massachusetts Institute of Technology study found that on Twitter, fake news stories are 70 percent more likely than real stories to get retweeted.
- In a 2018 poll of people from thirty-seven countries by YouGov for the Reuters Institute for the Study of Journalism, only 23 percent said they trusted the news on social media.
- In a 2018 Pew Research Center survey, 56 percent of adults in the United States wanted technology companies to take steps to restrict fake news.
- In May, June, and early July 2018, Twitter removed an average of 1 million fake accounts per day.
- In July 2018 Facebook announced that it would not remove fake content but would demote it.

Related Organizations and Websites

Brookings Institution
1775 Massachusetts Ave. NW
Washington, DC 20036
email: communications@brookings.edu
website: www.brookings.edu

This liberal think tank conducts research aimed at solving problems in society. Research areas include foreign policy, economics, development, and governance. The organization has studied fake news.

Center for Media Literacy (CML)
22603 Pacific Coast Hwy., #549
Malibu, CA 90265
email: cml@medialit.com
website: www.medialit.org

The CML provides resources on media literacy education and professional development to people in the United States and abroad. The organization's goal is to help people develop critical-thinking and media-production skills, which it claims can help people avoid falling for fake news.

Freedom House
1850 M St. NW, Eleventh Floor
Washington, DC 20036
email: info@freedomhouse.org
website: https://freedomhouse.org

Freedom House promotes open government and freedom of information and ideas. One of its programs focuses on Internet freedom and seeks to prevent governments from abusing their power in order to limit free speech.

Kettering Foundation
200 Commons Rd.
Dayton, OH 45459
email: info@kettering.org
website: www.kettering.org

This nonprofit organization conducts research exploring the question of what it takes to make democracy work as it should. This research especially focuses on how people can work together to address problems such as fake news.

Knight Foundation
200 S. Biscayne Blvd., Suite 3300
Miami, FL 33131
website: https://knightfoundation.org

The Knight Foundation supports journalism and the arts with the goal of keeping communities engaged and informed. The organization's focus on journalism includes support for free expression and journalistic excellence.

National Association for Media Literacy Education
PO Box 343
New York, NY 10024
email: namle@namle.net
website: https://namle.net

The goal of this organization is to promote media literacy as an essential life skill and help teach people the critical-thinking and communication abilities they need in order to be active, thoughtful citizens.

News Literacy Project
5335 Wisconsin Ave. NW, Suite 440
Washington, DC 20015
website: https://newslit.org

This organization offers programs that teach students the skills they need to become smart news consumers and active participants in democracy.

Poynter Institute
801 Third St. S.
St. Petersburg, FL 33701
email: info@poynter.org
website: www.poynter.org

The Poynter Institute provides journalism instruction and resources to promote freedom of expression and democracy. The institute's goal is to prepare journalists to hold powerful people accountable and spread honest information.

For Further Research

Books

Donald A. Barclay, *Fake News, Propaganda, and Plain Old Lies: How to Find Trustworthy Information in the Digital Age*. Lanham, MD: Rowman & Littlefield, 2018.

Stephen Currie, *Sharing Posts: The Spread of Fake News*. San Diego, CA: ReferencePoint, 2018.

Michiko Kakutani, *The Death of Truth: Notes on Falsehood in the Age of Trump*. New York: Duggan, 2018.

Daniel Levitin, *Weaponized Lies: How to Think Critically in the Post-truth Era*. Boston: Dutton, 2017.

Carla Mooney, *Fake News and the Manipulation of Public Opinion*. San Diego, CA: ReferencePoint, 2019.

Internet Sources

Janna Anderson and Lee Rainie, "The Future of Truth and Misinformation Online," Pew Research Center, October 19, 2017. www.pewresearch.org.

Alison J. Head et al., "How Students Engage with News," Knight Foundation, October 16, 2018. https://knightfoundation.org.

Katie Langin, "Fake News Spreads Faster than True News on Twitter—Thanks to People, Not Bots," *Science*, March 8, 2018. www.sciencemag.org.

Carli V. Lowe, "Fake News or Free Speech: Is There a Right to be Misinformed?," *American Libraries*, June 25, 2018. https://americanlibraries magazine.org.

Katharine Viner, "A Mission for Journalism in a Time of Crisis," *Guardian* (Manchester), November 16, 2017. www.theguardian.com.

Darrell M. West, "How to Combat Fake News and Disinformation," Brookings Institution, December 18, 2017. www.brookings.edu.

Index

About the Author

Kathryn Hulick began her career with an adventure. She served two years in the Peace Corps in Kyrgyzstan, teaching English. When she returned to the United States, she began writing books and articles for kids. Technology and science are her favorite topics. Look for her books: *Cyber Nation*, *Cybersecurity Careers*, and *How Robotics Is Changing the World*. She also contributes regularly to *Muse* magazine and the Science News for Students website. She lives in Massachusetts with her husband and son.